Creole and Cajun Cookbook

The Ultimate Source for Easy, Authentic and Delicious Recipes

By

Angel Burns

© 2021 Angel Burns, All Rights Reserved.

License Notices

This book or parts thereof might not be reproduced in any format for personal or commercial use without the written permission of the author. Possession and distribution of this book by any means without said permission is prohibited by law.

All content is for entertainment purposes and the author accepts no responsibility for any damages, commercially or personally, caused by following the content.

Table of Contents

Introduction 7

What is Cajun 9

What is Creole 10

Breakfast 13

    Louisiana Cajun Crab Cakes 14

    Cajun Fries 16

    Creole Stuffed Shrimp 19

    Cajun Couche Couche 22

    Shrimp Po'Boy Sliders 24

    Creole Cream Cheese with Fresh Fruit and Cane Syrup 27

    Cajun Shrimp Enchiladas 29

    Cajun Fried Pickles 32

    Cajun & Creole Seafood Dip 35

    Eggs Hussard 37

    Eggs Creole 40

    Cajun Breakfast Skillet 42

Egg & Sausage Pie 44

Spicy Sausage Breakfast Casserole 47

Cajun Citrus Shrimp 50

Cajun Pasta Chicken 53

Louisiana Breakfast Rice 56

Pecan & Sweet Potato Waffles 59

Lunch 61

Cajun Shrimp with Corn & Bell Peppers 62

New Orleans BBQ Shrimp 65

Red Beans and Rice with Ground Beef 67

Cajun Rice Bake 69

Cajun Sausage Chicken Gumbo 72

Easy Shrimp & Sausage Gumbo 75

Chicken Étouffée 78

Louisiana Alligator Style Creole Stew 81

Gumbo 84

Blackened Fish 87

Cornbread Stuffed Pork Loin on the Grill 89

- Rabbit Smothered in Sauce 93
- Cheesy Shrimp and Grits.. 96
- Cajun Brisket... 99
- Crispy Cajun Shrimp 102
- Fried Soft Shell Crab 104

Dinner 107

- Cajun Chicken 108
- Cajun BBQ Chicken 110
- Shrimp, Sausage, And Grits 113
- Shrimp And Andouille Dirty Rice 116
- Cajun Shrimp Kebabs... 119
- Fried Catfish Nuggets... 121
- Buffalo Shrimp 124
- Beer-Battered Cajun Fried Fish.. 127
- Court-Bouillon 129
- Cajun Beef Stew.. 132
- Southern Fried Chicken.. 135
- Parmesan-Crusted Pork Chops 137

Creole Okra Shrimp 139

Creole Collard Greens 142

Oyster Bacon Gumbo 145

Red Snapper 148

Cajun Honey Chicken Wings 150

Cajun Salmon 152

Cajun Seared Scallops 154

Conclusion 156

Author's Afterthoughts 157

Introduction

You have probably heard of Louisiana, but do you know where it is? Most people recognize the name "New Orleans" but don't know the area's rich history or what types of foods are served in its restaurants. If you have ever wanted to try a taste of Louisiana, this cookbook is for you!

In the past two decades, Cajun and Creole food has been growing in popularity around the world. Originated from French settlers who came to Louisiana in 1719, this cuisine is part of a hybrid cuisine that includes Caribbean influences as well as those from other cultures like Spanish and African. A staple of Louisiana's culture, Cajun and Creole cooking can be found almost anywhere you go, whether it is a restaurant or an everyday event.

The term "Cajun" refers to a group of Acadian refugees who settled in Louisiana in the late 18th century after being expelled from Canada. The term "Creole" refers to the people born in Louisiana who are descendants of Europeans, Africans, and Native Americans. Therefore, Cajun and Creole are not two distinct cuisines but one.

What is Cajun

Most scholars classify Cajuns as an ethnic group descended from Acadians. Acadians are French immigrants who settled in Canada. In the late 1700s, they were expelled and moved to lower Louisiana, where they would become known as Cajuns. Cajuns are renowned for their colorful music (including Zydeco), energetic dancing, and delectable cuisine. They can be easily recognized by their distinct Cajun-French accents.

What is Creole

Creole is a concept that is more difficult to describe than Cajun and has no official meaning. Historians have characterized Creole as ranging from an ethnic group made up of people of European, African, Caribbean, and Hispanic descent to people of French or Spanish heritage who were born in New Orleans. It is clear that Creole culture and heritage have left their mark on New Orleans in a variety of ways. Creole contributions can be found in many aspects of New Orleans' culture, art, food, and more.

Cajun food tends to be spicier and more highly seasoned than its counterpart Creole food. In addition, Cajun food uses different ingredients than Creole food. Therefore, you will find differences in the two cuisines, like in the types of meat used. Cajun food uses pork and beef instead of chicken and fish. This is because pork and beef are more available in Louisiana. In Creole cuisine, however, you will find a high variety of seafood combined with vegetables and seasonings like garlic, onions, celery, bell peppers, etc. In addition, Cajun food uses more beans, tomatoes, and corn.

Creole food is also known as New Orleans food or Louisiana Creole cuisine. The French settlers who came to Louisiana first settled in the St. Louis parish of Louisiana, where they had a large sugar cane plantation and sugar refinery. Being Specialize in seafood, Creole cuisine has ancient origins, but it did not gain popularity until the early 20th century when new immigrants from different regions across America started experimenting with local foods. Creole cuisine uses different seasonings like nutmeg, mace, and allspice as opposed to Cajun food which uses spices like cayenne pepper and thyme. The dishes are also more sophisticated due to the influence of other cultures. A great example of this is the use of raw oysters in gumbo, which only happens in Creole cooking.

Although these two cuisines are generally different from each other in various ways, they do share some similarities as well. The biggest similarity is that these two cuisines use many of the same ingredients. Some of the ingredients used in Cajun cooking are known as traditional or expected items, such as onions, bell peppers, celery, tomatoes, flour, and salt. In Creole foods, you will find other ingredients like coconut milk, salt pork (cured pork), rice, red beans, and okra. Also, when Creole food received its name was due to its distinct flavor from other Louisiana food.

Cajun and Creole foods can be considered a culinary fusion. Over the centuries, Cajun and Creole cuisines have adapted to each other's traditions by becoming more diversified. This has led to some similarities in ingredients, preparation techniques, and seasonings.

By comparing the two cuisines, you can see why they are both distinct in the way they taste, even though they use a lot of similar ingredients. This can be attributed to the different populations that live in Louisiana and the differences between the groups. Because of this, their cuisines reflect their diverse cultures.

Cajun and Creole food can easily be given a place in your diet due to their wide variety of dishes. They are tasty, spicy, filling, and versatile. Cajun and Creole food contribute to the unique flavors of Louisiana's cuisine. They also are a great way to experience the rich culture of the state.

Creole and Cajun cooking traditions date back hundreds of years. There are hundreds of dishes to be experienced, and they are all waiting for you in this cookbook! This book will teach you how to prepare some of Louisiana's most popular dishes. You can enjoy the best that Louisiana has to offer with the Creole and Cajun Cookbook!

The Creole and Cajun Cookbook is the ultimate resource for anyone who is looking to feed themselves or their family with delicious and hearty meals. There are so many ways to use this book, you can learn how to cook traditional recipes from the South, or you can alter them slightly to give them your own twist. Either way, you can use this book to your advantage.

Breakfast

Start your day with delicious food to make the rest of your day the best! Enjoy the morning by making these southern dishes. The first meal of the day has never been so tasty.

Louisiana Cajun Crab Cakes

Crab cakes are great for a fun twist on the classic. These Louisiana-style crab cakes are light and delicious.

Servings: 6

Preparation Time: 35 minutes

Ingredients:

- 2 tbsp. bread crumbs, dried
- 8 oz. lump crabmeat, (snow crab or blue crab)
- 2 tsp. Dijon-style mustard
- ¼ c. mayonnaise
- 8 oz. shrimp, cooked & finely chopped
- ½ tsp. Tabasco sauce
- 2 tsp. Worcestershire sauce
- ⅛ tsp. Cajun spice mix
- 2 tbsp. or more vegetable oil
- 1 large egg
- 2 tbsp. parsley, fresh, minced
- 1½ c. corn chips, crushed or panko breadcrumbs
- 2 tsp. bottled horseradish
- Cayenne pepper & salt to taste

Instructions:

Combine all the ingredients together (except the panko or corn chips & vegetable oil) in a large bowl.

Form the mixture into 12 round cakes (2x½") & pat the crushed panko or chips on the crab cakes, both sides.

Now, over medium heat in a large non-stick skillet, heat the oil & sauté the crab cakes until golden & hot throughout, for 2 to 3 minutes per side.

Cajun Fries

Cajun fries are cooked to perfection and topped with just the right spice to make them the ultimate snack.

Servings: 4

Preparation Time: 45 minutes

Ingredients:

- 4 potatoes, medium, peeled & sliced into French fry shapes
- ½ tsp. onion powder
- ⅛ tsp. black pepper
- ¼ tsp. oregano
- 1 tsp. paprika
- ⅛ tsp. cayenne or to taste
- ¼ tsp. Tabasco sauce
- ¼ tsp. cumin
- 1 tsp. garlic powder
- ¼ tsp. thyme
- 1 tbsp. vegetable oil
- ¼ tsp. sugar
- ½ tsp. salt

Instructions:

Preheat your oven to 400 F in advance.

Combine oregano together with thyme, paprika, cayenne, black pepper, garlic powder, cumin, sugar, salt, Tabasco sauce, onion powder & oil in a small bowl; mix well until you get a paste with consistency. Pour a small amount of oil on a baking sheet lined with aluminum foil; spread with a paper towel.

Place the fries in a plastic bag with paste; shake well until evenly coated with the paste. Now, place the fries on the lined baking sheet, ensure they don't touch each other.

Bake in the preheated oven for 30 to 35 minutes; to brown the underside, don't forget to turn them once during the cooking process.

Creole Stuffed Shrimp

Creole stuffed shrimp is a light and delicious meal that will soon become your family's favorite. When you go out to dine, you order Stuffed Shrimp because you think it's too difficult to cook at home. You'll enjoy making this no-fuss meal because it's so easy, but best of all, your family and guests will praise you profusely.

Servings: 4

Preparation Time: 1 hour and 5 minutes

Ingredients:

For Shrimp:

- 12 jumbo shrimp, peeled, deveined & butterflied
- ½ c. celery, diced
- 1 c. kielbasa, diced
- ½ c. chicken broth, low sodium
- 2 tsp. Creole seasoning
- 6 tbsp. butter, unsalted, divided
- 1 c. diced onion
- 4 tbsp. parsley, fresh & minced
- ½ c. dry white wine or ½ c. dry sherry
- 2 cloves garlic, minced
- ½ c. red bell pepper or ½ c. green bell peppers, diced
- 2 c. butter-flavored crackers, coarsely crushed
- Ground pepper & salt to taste

For Sauce:

- 4 tbsp. scallions, minced
- 2 tbsp. honey
- 4 tbsp. mayonnaise
- 2 tbsp. chicken broth
- 4 tbsp. grainy mustard
- Juice of 1 lemon, fresh

Instructions:

Lightly coat a baking dish using your cooking spray & preheat your oven to 425 F.

Melt 2 tbsp. of butter in a skillet, over medium-high heat, and then add in the kielbasa. Sauté until the kielbasa starts to brown, for 3 minutes. Add in the celery, Creole seasoning, onion, bell pepper, and garlic; continue sautéing until the veggies become soft, for 5 more minutes.

Deglaze your skillet using wine or sherry; let simmer until a large percentage of the liquid manages to evaporate. Take from heat & add in ½ cup of broth, crushed crackers & parsley—season with pepper & salt to taste.

Mound the stuffing to every prepared shrimp, pressing over the top of the shrimp tail. Place the stuffed shrimp into the ready baking dish. Ensure you melt the leftover butter & drizzle it on the shrimp's top. Bake until the shrimp is cooked through, for 12 minutes.

For Sauce: Combine all the sauce ingredients together in a bowl; mix well.

For Serving: Evenly divide your sauce among 4 plates. Top each sauce with 3 stuffed shrimp.

Cajun Couche Couche

Couche Couche is another unique application of the typical Louisiana style of cooking. This dish is easy to make and full of flavor.

Servings: 4

Preparation Time: 35 minutes

Ingredients:

- 1 tsp. baking powder
- 2 c. yellow cornmeal
- 1 c. water
- 2 tbsp. cooking oil
- 1 tsp. salt

Instructions:

Mix cornmeal together with baking powder, water, and salt; ensure the mixture is not too dry. If required, feel free to add more water.

Place the mixture into hot oil & cook in a heavy pot or cast iron. Allow the mixture to form a "crust" at the bottom of the pot.

Give everything a good stir & then decrease the heat; let simmer.

Cover & cook for 20 minutes, stirring every now and then.

Serve with syrup and/or milk.

Shrimp Po'Boy Sliders

Sliders are a great way to enjoy different types of cuisine. These Shrimp Po'Boy Sliders are bursting with flavor and the perfect meal for a party. These mini sandwiches can feed a dozen people. One slider can give you full satisfaction with its tons of flavors rolled into one. The spicy, tangy, and creamy remoulade is spread on the bun, topped with fried shrimp, lettuce, and cherry tomatoes.

Servings: 12

Preparation Time: 5 minutes

Ingredients:

- 2 large eggs
- 1/2 c. whole milk
- 1/2 c. finely ground cornmeal
- 1/2 c. all-purpose flour
- 1 tsp. dried thyme
- 1 tbsp. Cajun seasoning
- Freshly ground black pepper
- Kosher salt
- 1 lb. peeled & deveined shrimp, tails removed
- Vegetable oil, for frying
- 12 slider buns

For serving:

- Sliced cherry tomatoes
- Shredded iceberg lettuce

For the remoulade:

- 1 tbsp. whole-grain mustard
- 1 c. mayonnaise
- 1 tbsp. Louisiana hot sauce
- 1 tbsp. lemon juice
- 2 thinly sliced green onions
- 1 tbsp. chopped parsley

Instructions:

Whisk in a large bowl the eggs and milk. Set aside.

Whisk in another large bowl the cornmeal, flour, dried thyme, and Cajun seasoning; season with salt and black pepper.

Dredge the shrimp in the egg-milk mixture, tossing in the flour mixture to coat.

Heat about two-inch of oil in a large skillet over medium heat.

When the oil is shimmering, fry the shrimp for two minutes on each side until golden and drain on a plate lined with a paper towel.

Prepare the remoulade by whisking in a bowl the mayonnaise, green onions, mustard, parsley, hot sauce, and lemon juice.

Assemble the sliders by spreading the remoulade on the bottom bun.

Top with fried shrimp, and then lettuce and tomatoes.

Finally, cover with slider bun tops.

Serve!

Creole Cream Cheese with Fresh Fruit and Cane Syrup

Cream Cheese is a timeless favorite, and a unique combination of creole dishes can make cream cheese even more delicious.

Servings: 4

Preparation Time: 30 minutes

Ingredients:

- 6 c. skim milk
- ⅓ c. buttermilk
- ½ tablet rennet
- 3 c. fresh strawberries, blueberries, or sliced fresh peaches
- 6 tbsp. Steen's Cane Syrup

Instructions:

In a medium stainless-steel saucepan over medium-low heat, combine the skim milk, buttermilk, and rennet tablet. Heat the mixture to 105°F and hold it there for about 5 minutes.

Remove the pan from the heat, cover with cheesecloth, and allow to sit at room temperature for at least 3 hours and up to 24 hours.

Place a colander lined with a double layer of cheesecloth in the sink and gently ladle the curds into the colander. Allow draining for at least 1 hour until the curds form into one solid piece. Discard the remaining whey and liquid from the pot. Transfer the cheese to a container and refrigerate until ready to use.

To serve, divide the cheese evenly among 6 bowls. Top each bowl with ½ c. of the fruit and drizzle with 1 tbsp. of the cane syrup.

Cajun Shrimp Enchiladas

Enchiladas are a great way to include a little extra flavor in your meal. Cajun shrimp enchiladas are a great meal that is perfect for you or your whole family. One bite of this delicious dish, and I know you will be hooked. This is a dish that can be served alone or alongside a side of rice or pasta.

Servings: 4-6

Preparation Time: 30 minutes

Ingredients:

- 1 onion, chopped
- 3 cloves garlic, minced
- 2 tbsp. extra virgin olive oil
- 3 lb. shrimp, peeled and deveined
- 2 tbsp. Cajun seasoning
- 1 c. heavy whipping cream
- 2 tbsp. cornstarch, mixed with 1 tbsp. of cold water
- 10 (5 inches) flour tortillas

Instructions:

Place a large frying pan over medium heat. Add in the olive oil. Once hot, add in the minced garlic and chopped onion. Stir well to mix and cook for 5 minutes or until soft.

Add in the shrimp and Cajun seasoning. Toss to mix. Cook for 1 to 2 minutes or until the shrimp begins to turn pink.

Add in the heavy whipping cream and bring to a simmer. Add in the cornstarch and water mixture. Whisk until evenly mixed. Cook for 1 to 2 minutes or until the mixture is thick consistently.

Preheat the oven to 325 degrees.

Pour the spoon into a large baking dish. Spoon the shrimp into the center of the flour tortillas. Roll tightly and place into the baking dish with the seam side facing down. Cover with a sheet of aluminum foil.

Place into the oven to bake for 15 to 20 minutes.

Remove and serve immediately.

Cajun Fried Pickles

Fried pickles are a Texas favorite. Preparing them at home is easy, and they taste wonderful.

Servings: 4

Preparation Time: 30 minutes

Ingredients:

- 1 c. all-purpose flour
- 1 ½ tsp. Cajun seasoning
- ¾ tsp. powdered garlic
- ½ tsp. salt
- ¼ tsp. black pepper
- 2 tbsp. hot sauce
- 1 c. buttermilk
- 16 oz. dill pickle chips, drained and dried

Ingredients for the garlic and blue cheese sauce:

- ½ c. buttermilk
- ¼ c. mayonnaise
- ¼ c. sour cream
- 1 tbsp. lemon juice
- ¼ tsp. hot sauce
- 1 clove garlic, minced
- ¼ tsp. salt
- 1/8 tsp. black pepper
- ¼ c. parsley, chopped
- 2 tbsp. chives, chopped
- ½ c. blue cheese, crumbled

Instructions:

Add all of the ingredients for the blue cheese sauce into a blender except for the crumbled blue cheese itself. Blend on the highest setting until smooth consistency.

Add in the crumbled blue cheese and pulse again until slightly chunky.

Pour into a container and set aside in the fridge until ready to serve.

Line a large baking sheet with a few paper towels.

Place a large pot over medium to high heat. Pour in 2 inches of vegetable oil. Heat the oil until it reaches 385 degrees.

In a medium bowl, add in the all-purpose flour, Cajun seasoning, powdered garlic, black pepper, a dash of salt, hot sauce, and buttermilk. Whisk well until smooth consistency.

Blot the dill pickles dry with a paper towel. Transfer into the batter and toss to coat. Immediately drop them into the hot oil. Fry for 1 to 3 minutes or until golden brown. Remove and place onto a large plate lined with a few paper towels.

Serve the pickles with the premade blue cheese sauce.

Cajun & Creole Seafood Dip

Seafood dips are a favorite for many. This Cajun & Creole Seafood Dip is sure to be a hit with any crowd. We can find a reason to host a celebration for almost everything. Dips are an easy, delightful treat for hungry guests when there's a bunch to feed.

Servings: 6

Preparation Time: 35 minutes

Ingredients:

- ½ lb. imitation crabmeat
- ½ tbsp. Cajun seasoning
- ⅓ c. sour cream
- 8 oz. cream cheese, softened
- ½ tsp. Italian seasoning
- 1 tbsp. hot sauce
- ½ tbsp. Worcestershire sauce
- ½ c. cheddar cheese, shredded
- 1 bunch of green onion, sliced thinly
- ½ tsp. garlic powder

Instructions:

Mix sour cream together with cream cheese, Cajun Seasoning, Worcestershire Sauce, hot sauce, Italian seasoning, and garlic with an electric mixer or in a food processor.

Gently fold in the crab, cheddar cheese, and onions.

Refrigerate for a minimum period of 2 hours & adjust the seasonings to your taste.

Eggs Hussard

Eggs Hussard is a delicious breakfast dish that will soon become a family favorite. This dish allows you to be creative with your cooking and create wonderful recipes.

Servings: 4

Preparation Time: 57 minutes

Ingredients:

- 8 Canadian bacon slices
- ¼ yellow onion, chopped finely
- 2 c. plus 3 tbsp. butter, unsalted
- ¼ c. ham, chopped finely
- 1 garlic clove, chopped finely
- ½ tsp. thyme, dried
- 1 scallion, fresh, chopped finely
- ¼ c. mushrooms, minced
- 1 tbsp. all-purpose flour
- ¾ c. beef stock
- 8 Holland rusks
- ¼ c. dry red wine
- 2 tsp. Worcestershire sauce
- ¼ c. parsley, fresh, chopped finely
- 1 bay leaf
- ⅓ c. Parmesan cheese, grated
- 4 egg yolks, plus 8 poached eggs, for serving
- 1 ½ tsp. red wine vinegar
- ¼ tsp. cayenne pepper, plus more for serving
- 1 tomato, medium, cut into 4 slices
- Freshly ground black pepper & kosher salt to taste

Instructions:

Over medium-high heat in a 2-quart saucepan, heat approximately 2 tbsp. of butter. Add in the scallions, garlic & onions; cook for 2 to 3 minutes, until soft. Add mushrooms & ham; cook for 3 to 4 minutes. Add in the flour; cook for a minute, stirring. Add in the wine, stock, thyme, Worcestershire, & bay leaf; bring everything together to a boil. Once boiling, decrease the heat to medium & briefly cook until slightly thick. Stir in 2 tbsp. of parsley & season with pepper and salt; keep warm.

Now, over medium-low heat in a 2-quart saucepan; heat 2 c. of butter. Skim & discard the film from the surface. Transfer the clarified butter from the pan into a large bowl, leaving the milky sediment behind. Fill a 4-quart saucepan with 2 inches of water; bring it to a simmer over medium heat & rest a heatproof bowl over the pan. Add in the egg yolks, cayenne, vinegar & 1 tsp. of water to the boil; cook for 4 to 5 minutes, until a thick sauce has formed, whisking constantly. Start adding the clarified butter in a thin stream, whisking; until you have utilized all the butter and the hollandaise is completely smooth.

Heat your oven to broil. Arrange the tomato slices on a large baking sheet. Season with pepper and salt; sprinkle with cheese & broil for a couple of minutes, until the cheese is melted & browned; set aside.

Heat the leftover butter over medium heat in a 12" skillet. Add in the bacon; cook for several minutes until warmed. Evenly divide the rusks among 4 plates, putting a bacon slice on each. Spoon approximately 2 tbsp. of the red wine sauce on top of the bacon, & top with a poached egg.

Spoon the hollandaise on top of the eggs. Garnish your plates with tomatoes, leftover parsley & more cayenne.

Eggs Creole

Eggs Creole is another delicious breakfast dish you will love. It is easy to prepare and bursting with flavor.

Servings: 12

Preparation Time: 8 hours and 30 minutes

Ingredients:

- 2 lb. shrimp, large, cooked, peeled & deveined
- ½ c. ketchup
- 4 green onions, chopped
- ½ c. tomato puree
- 1 onion, small, chopped
- ½ c. red wine vinegar
- 4 celery stalks, chopped coarsely
- ½ c. Creole mustard
- 12 lettuce leaves, fresh
- 1 ⅛ c. vegetable oil
- 2 tsp. paprika
- ¾ c. Italian flat leaf parsley, fresh
- 1 tsp. Worcestershire sauce

Instructions:

Pulse celery together with green onions, parsley & onion in a food processor until chopped finely, on high settings. Add in the tomato puree, ketchup, vinegar, Worcestershire sauce & mustard. Process it on high settings again until blended well, scraping down the sides of your bowl few times.

With the food processor still running, drizzle the oil in a steady stream & process until blended. Stir in the paprika. Transfer the mixture to a large bowl. Cover & let refrigerate overnight or for a minimum period of 6 to 8 hours.

When ready, give the sauce a good stir, then transfer on top of the shrimp; toss several times until evenly coated. Serve over the lettuce leaves.

Cajun Breakfast Skillet

Breakfast Skillets are not only easy to prepare, but they are also delicious and bursting with flavor. This breakfast includes jambalaya seasoning, which complements the sausage and eggs. It's a wonderful morning dish.

Servings: 6

Preparation Time: 35 minutes

Ingredients:

- 1/2 lb. sausage, lean
- 1/2 c. mixed bell peppers and onions, chopped
- 1 pkg. jambalaya seasoning mix
- 6 eggs, large
- 1/2 c. milk, 2%
- 1/4 c. cheese shreds

Instructions:

Cook the sausage with pepper and onion mixture in a large-sized skillet.

Combine the milk, eggs, and seasoning mix in a medium bowl.

When the mixture has cooked thoroughly, add the egg mixture and cook on med. Heat. As eggs start setting, stir the mixture gently. Continue cooking while occasionally stirring till eggs have set completely. Remove pan from burner and sprinkle mixture with cheese. Serve in burritos or as breakfast bowls.

Egg & Sausage Pie

This egg and sausage pie is a great dish that is easy to make and sure to be a hit with your family. It makes your morning meal become a celebration to start the day.

Servings: 4

Preparation Time: 2 hours and 5 minutes

Ingredients:

- 14 eggs, large
- 1 c. half 'n half
- 4 x 1"-thick slices of French bread, day old
- 1 tbsp. oil, canola
- 1 c. bulk sausage, any type
- 1 c. diced onions, yellow
- 2 tbsp. sliced tops from green onions
- 1 tbsp. garlic, minced
- 1 tbsp. chopped rosemary, fresh
- 1 x 10-oz. can drained diced tomatoes with green chilies, mild
- 1 tbsp. sauce, hot
- Cooking spray
- 2 thinly sliced small tomatoes, red
- 1 c. canned or jarred, drained, sliced bell peppers, yellow and red
- 2 tbsp. chopped cilantro, fresh
- 1 tbsp. diced jalapeno, fresh
- Salt, kosher
- Pepper, freshly ground
- To garnish: rosemary sprigs, fresh

Instructions:

Preheat oven to 350 degrees F.

Crack eggs into a large-sized bowl. Add milk. Whisk till combined fully. Add sliced bread and immerse it fully in the mixture. Allow soaking for an hour.

In an iron skillet on med heat, add sausage. Sauté till fully cooked and browned, rendering out the fat. This takes 10 minutes or so. Remove pieces of sausage to the platter.

In the same iron skillet, add onions to the remainder of the fat. Sauté till they are translucent, five minutes or so. Add rosemary, green onions, and garlic. Sauté for a minute.

Add and stir in green chilies and tomatoes, along with the hot sauce. Turn heat off. Pour excess grease out of the skillet. Add mixture to a platter of sausage. Rinse skillet. Wipe it dry.

Use cooking spray on the skillet. Place four bread slices in it. Pour egg mixture over them. Spoon sausage and vegetable mixture into egg mixture bread.

Lay tomatoes and peppers throughout the mixture randomly. Sprinkle jalapenos and cilantro around the mixture. Season as desired.

Place in oven. Bake for 30-45 minutes till eggs have set and a knife blade inserted comes back clean.

Slice portions of bread mixture. Place on the plate(s). Use rosemary to garnish. Serve.

Spicy Sausage Breakfast Casserole

Sausage is a great way to add some extra flavor to your breakfast. This Spicy Sausage Breakfast Casserole is bursting with flavor.

Servings: 6

Preparation Time: 60 minutes

Ingredients:

- 12-16 oz. thinly sliced andouille sausage, smoked
- 1/2 c. onion, chopped
- 1/2 c. chopped bell pepper, green or red
- 6 eggs, large
- 1 1/2 c. milk, whole
- 1 tsp. seasoning blend, Cajun or Creole
- 1/4 tsp. pepper, ground
- Optional: 1 tbsp. chopped parsley, fresh
- Salt, kosher pepper, ground
- 4 bread slices, torn in 1" pieces
- 2 diced tomatoes, medium
- 2 c. cheddar cheese shreds

Instructions:

Heat the oven to 350 degrees F. Butter 2-quart, shallow baking dish evenly.

Cook sausage with bell pepper and onion in a large-sized skillet till the vegetables become translucent. Whisk the eggs and milk in a medium bowl with seasoning and parsley. Then, season as desired and set the bowl aside.

Arrange bread pieces on the bottom of a baking dish. Sprinkle with diced tomatoes and sausage mixture. Add cheese and pour the egg mixture over the top evenly—season as desired.

Bake casserole for 35-40 minutes, till browned lightly and puffy. Serve.

There are all kinds of spicy, enticing Cajun recipes for lunch, dinner, side dishes, and appetizers. Try one soon…

Cajun Citrus Shrimp

Citrus shrimp is a great example of the versatility of the Cajun kitchen. This dish is bursting with flavor and sure to be a hit. This dish presents itself beautifully, and you'll love the citrus flavor. The sauce adds a delicious touch to the recipe.

Servings: 10-12

Preparation Time: 40 minutes

Ingredients:

- 2 halved lemons, fresh
- 2 halved limes, fresh
- 1/4 orange, fresh
- 1 tbsp. red pepper, crushed
- 4 lb. fresh shrimp, large, unpeeled
- 2 c. orange juice, freshly squeezed
- 2 c. pineapple juice
- 2 c. grapefruit juice
- 1/2 c. lime juice, fresh
- 1/2 c. lemon juice, fresh
- 1 sliced orange
- 1 sliced lemon
- 1 sliced grapefruit
- 1 sliced lime
- 1 tsp. dried red pepper, crushed
- Leaves of lettuce
- Louis sauce, prepared
- For Garnishing: sliced citrus fruits

Instructions:

Combine salted water, lemon halves, and the next three ingredients in a large pot. Bring to boil. Add the shrimp. Cook for two to three minutes till shrimp are barely pink. Plunge the shrimp into iced water to halt the cooking process and drain.

Peel the shrimp and leave the tails on. Devein, as desired.

Combine the orange juice and next nine ingredients in a shallow, large dish. Add the shrimp. Cover dish and chill for 25 minutes. Drain liquid off. Garnish as desired. Serve the shrimp on lettuce with prepared Louis sauce.

Cajun Pasta Chicken

This Cajun pasta chicken dish is simple to make and sure to be a hit with your family.

Servings: 4

Preparation Time: 25 minutes

Ingredients:

- 12 oz. linguine, uncooked
- 2 lb. strips, chicken breast
- 1 tbsp. seasoning, Cajun
- 1 1/4 tsp. salt, kosher
- 1/4 c. butter, unsalted
- 1 thinly sliced small bell pepper, red
- 1 thinly sliced small bell pepper, green
- 1 x 8-oz. pkg. of mushrooms, fresh
- 2 sliced green onions, only light green and white parts
- 1 1/2 c. half 'n half
- 1/4 tsp. pepper, lemon
- 1/4 tsp. basil, dried
- 1/4 tsp. garlic powder
- For Garnishing: green onions, chopped

Instructions:

Prepare the pasta using instructions on the package.

Evenly sprinkle chicken with 1 tsp. of salt and the Cajun seasoning. Melt 1/4 c. of butter in non-stick, large skillet on med-high. Add the chicken. Sauté for five to six minutes, till done, and remove the chicken.

Add peppers, green onions, and mushrooms to the skillet. Sauté for nine or 10 minutes, till liquid evaporates and vegetables become tender.

Return the chicken to skillet. Stir in the half 'n half and the next three ingredients, then last 1/4 tsp. of salt. Often stir while cooking on med-low for three to four minutes, till heated thoroughly. Add the linguine and coat by tossing. Garnish if you like. Serve promptly.

Louisiana Breakfast Rice

Louisiana Breakfast Rice is a great dish that can be served many different ways. It is easy to prepare and delicious.

Servings: 8-9

Preparation Time: 35 minutes

Ingredients:

- 1 cored, de-seeded, diced bell pepper, green
- 1 chopped onion, sweet
- Salt, coarse
- Black pepper, ground
- 3/4 c. tomato sauce
- 4 c. white rice, cooked
- 3 chopped garlic cloves
- 3 chopped green onions
- 3 sliced ribs of celery
- 2 tbsp. oil, canola
- 1 lb. sliced sausage, smoked
- 2 sprigs thyme leaves, fresh
- 2 chopped sage leaves, fresh
- 4 chopped basil leaves, fresh
- 1 tsp. paprika, ground
- 1 tbsp. fresh parsley, chopped
- Optional: Tabasco sauce

Instructions:

Heat skillet on med-high. Add sausage. Cook till the fat has been rendered, and sausage edges are dark brown and crisp. Use a slotted spoon to remove to warm plate. Keep it warm.

Add bell pepper, green onion, celery, and onion to skillet. Cook till vegetables have softened and onion becomes translucent. Add garlic. Cook till it is fragrant.

Add tomato sauce, rice, thyme, sage, basil, paprika, and parsley. Combine by stirring. If the mixture is too dry, just add 1/4 c. water. Stir until moist and combined well.

Reduce the heat to simmer. Cook till rice heats through. After that, return sausage to mixture. Taste. Add salt, pepper, and Tabasco sauce, if desired. Serve promptly.

Pecan & Sweet Potato Waffles

Pecan waffles and sweet potato waffles are a great combination for a delicious breakfast. This dish is sure to be a hit with any crowd. Among all the appealing Louisiana breakfasts, this may be your favorite treat for the morning meal. These waffles can even be repurposed as a dessert dish, topped with ice cream! Yum!

Servings: 4

Preparation Time: 5 minutes

Ingredients:

- 1/4 c. sugar, brown
- 4 lightly beaten eggs, large
- 6 tbsp. butter, melted
- 3/4 c. milk, 2%
- 1 c. sweet potato, boiled, then mashed
- 1 1/4 c. flour, all-purpose
- 1 c. pecans, chopped
- 2 tsp. baking powder
- 1/2 tsp. kosher salt

Instructions:

Toast pecans in a skillet on med. Heat. Stir frequently, till lightly toasted and fragrant.

Combine baking powder, flour, and salt in a small-sized bowl. Whisk and mix well.

Combine brown sugar, eggs, butter, milk, and sweet potato in a larger sized bowl. Mix by whisking. Add flour mixture and combine by stirring. Add pecans. Mix.

Cook mixture on preheated waffle iron till browned. Serve.

Lunch

The lunch meal is always something to look forward to. Give these recipes a try next time you are planning out your meals for the week. Your tastebuds will never be disappointed!

Cajun Shrimp with Corn & Bell Peppers

This Cajun shrimp with corn and bell peppers dish is bursting with flavor. It's so good it will steal the show, and you won't be disappointed.

Servings: 4

Preparation Time: 5 minutes

Ingredients:

- 2 tbsp. Divided olive oil
- ½ chopped onion
- 2 chopped bell peppers
- 2 minced cloves garlic
- 2/3 c. (frozen) corn, defrosted
- 1 ½ lb. peeled shrimp, deveined
- 2 tsp. Cajun seasoning
- Black pepper, freshly ground
- 1 tbsp. parsley, chopped
- 1 tbsp. lemon juice
- Kosher salt

Instructions:

Heat 1 tbsp. olive oil in a large pan on medium heat.

Sauté the bell peppers and onion for five minutes until tender.

Add the garlic and corn; cook for 1 minute longer. Transfer the mixture to a separate bowl. Set aside.

Heat the remaining one tbsp. oil using the same pan.

Place the shrimp in a single layer; season with Cajun seasoning, salt, and pepper. Cook for one to two minutes on each side until pink.

Add the vegetable mixture together with lemon juice, tossing to coat well. Sprinkle on top with parsley.

Serve!

New Orleans BBQ Shrimp

This New Orleans BBQ Shrimp is one delicious dish bursting with flavor. It's another dish that will have your guests coming back for more. New Orleans cuisine brings total satisfaction in every party. This BBQ shrimp makes your tongue drool with its fusion of buttery, tangy and spicy flavors from the mixture of hot sauce, Worcestershire sauce, beer, creole seasoning, and butter.

Servings: 2

Preparation Time: 5 minutes

Ingredients:

- 2 tbsp. butter
- 3 chopped cloves garlic
- 2 tsp. creole seasoning
- 1/4 c. Worcestershire sauce
- 1/4 c. hot sauce or more
- 2 tbsp. lemon juice of 1/2 lemon
- 1/3 c. beer, wine or broth
- 1/2 tsp. ground black pepper
- 1 lb. peeled and deveined shrimp
- 2 tbsp. chilled butter, cut into ½-inch pieces
- Salt to taste

Instructions:

In a pan, melt the butter on medium-high heat and sauté the garlic for 30 seconds until fragrant.

Stir in hot sauce, beer, Worcestershire sauce, lemon juice, pepper, and creole seasoning. Bring mixture to a simmer and cook for 5 to 7 minutes until half of the sauce is reduced.

Place the shrimp in the mixture and cook for 2 to 3 minutes on each side until cooked through. Simmer on medium-low and stir in cold butter until melted.

Sprinkle with salt if desired. Serve with French bread.

Enjoy!

Red Beans and Rice with Ground Beef

This Red Beans and Rice with Ground Beef is an easy and delicious dish that will have everyone ooh-ing and ahh-ing. It's another one of my favorites.

Servings: 8

Preparation Time: 5 minutes

Ingredients:

- 3 celery ribs
- 2 green peppers
- 2 tbsp. minced garlic
- 1 medium onion
- 1/4 c. bacon fat
- 2 tsp. Cajun seasoning
- 1 lb. ground beef
- 4 cans kidney beans
- 1 (14 oz.) package beef sausage
- 2 c. chicken or beef broth
- 8 c. hot cooked rice

Instructions:

Heat the oil in a 4-quart heavy-bottomed pot on medium heat.

Add the onion, garlic, bell pepper, and celery.

Cook the vegetables in bacon fat until softened. Stir in ground beef; cook until browned.

Add the beans and broth to the mixture. Stir in Cajun seasoning and bring to a boil.

Simmer on low heat and stir in sausage; simmer for half an hour. Top the cooked rice with beans.

Serve!

Cajun Rice Bake

This Cajun rice bake is so full of flavor that you will be kicking yourself for waiting so long to make it. It's one of the best recipes in this book.

Servings: 4

Preparation Time: 5 minutes

Ingredients:

- 1 tbsp. olive oil
- 2 minced cloves garlic
- 1/2 chopped red bell pepper
- 1/2 chopped green bell pepper
- 1 chopped medium onion
- 2 Andouille sausages
- 2 large chicken breasts
- 1 tsp. Cajun seasoning
- Freshly ground black pepper
- Kosher salt
- 1 1/4 c. long-grain white rice
- 2 c. chicken stock
- 1 (15 oz.) can tomato sauce
- 1 c. Cheddar cheese
- 3 sliced green onions

Instructions:

Preheat the oven to 375 degrees F.

Heat the olive oil in an ovenproof pan over medium heat.

Cook the bell peppers and onion in hot oil until starting to soften.

Cut the sausages into 1-inch pieces and add to the pan; cook until browned.

Add the garlic and sauté for 30 seconds until fragrant.

Cut the chicken breasts into 1-inch pieces and add to the pan along with Cajun seasoning. Season the mixture with salt and pepper; cook while you often stir until the chicken is thoroughly cooked.

Add the rice and pour over the chicken broth and tomato sauce and then stir in the cheddar. Simmer mixture and transfer to the oven.

Bake for 35 to 45 minutes until the rice is thoroughly cooked. Slightly cool the rice bake in the pan for five to ten minutes.

Sprinkle on top with sliced green onions.

Enjoy!

Cajun Sausage Chicken Gumbo

This Cajun Sausage Chicken Gumbo is the perfect blend of the traditional and the original. There isn't a secret trick to making great-tasting gumbo. As long as you follow the recipe and make it properly, you'll be amazed at how similar its taste is. This is what you might be served if you visit New Orleans.

Servings: 4-6

Preparation Time: 4 hours and 5 minutes

Ingredients:

- 1 lb. 1/4" sliced sausage, andouille
- 4 chicken breasts, bone-in, skin removed
- Oil, vegetable
- 3/4 c. flour, all-purpose
- 1 chopped onion, medium
- 1/2 chopped bell pepper, green
- 2 sliced ribs celery
- 2 quarts water, hot
- 3 minced cloves garlic
- 2 bay leaves, medium
- 1 tbsp. Worcestershire sauce, low sodium
- 2 tsp. seasoning, Creole
- 1/2 tsp. thyme, dried
- 1 tsp. sauce, hot
- 4 sliced green onions
- Cooked rice, hot
- For garnishing: green onions, chopped finely

Instructions:

Cook the sausage in a large pot on med. Heat and stir constantly for five minutes, or till the sausage browns. Drain it on a layer of paper towels and reserve the drippings in the pot. Set the sausage aside.

Cook the chicken in drippings in the pot on med. Heat for five minutes, till it browns. Place it on paper towels as well and reserve the drippings in the pot. Set the chicken aside.

Add oil to the drippings in the pot till you have 1/2 c. total. Add the flour. Cook on med. Heat and stir constantly for 20-25 minutes, till roux is the color of chocolate.

Add and stir in the celery, onion, and bell pepper. Stir often while cooking for seven or eight minutes, till the vegetables are tender. Add 2 quarts of hot water gradually. Bring the mixture to a boil.

Add the garlic, chicken, and next five ingredients. Reduce the heat level to low. Occasionally stir while simmering for an hour. Remove the chicken and allow it to cool.

Add the sausage to your gumbo and cook for 1/2 hour. Add and stir green onions and cook for 1/2 hour longer.

Debone the chicken. Cut meat in strips and return it to the gumbo. Simmer for five minutes. Remove the bay leaves and discard them.

Remove the gumbo from the burner. Garnish as desired and serve on cooked, hot rice.

Easy Shrimp & Sausage Gumbo

Easy Shrimp & Sausage Gumbo is perfect for a quick and easy lunch. It's a great dish to have on hand for busy days.

Servings: 4

Preparation Time: 25 minutes

Ingredients:

- 4 tbsp. butter
- 1/4 c. flour, all-purpose
- 1 chopped medium green bell pepper
- 1 small yellow onion
- 2 chopped celery ribs
- 12 oz. Andouille sausage, sliced into 1/2" pieces
- 2 minced cloves garlic
- Black pepper, freshly ground
- Kosher salt
- 1 tbsp. salt less Cajun seasoning
- 1 bay leaf
- 1 lb. peeled & deveined shrimp
- 15 oz. fire-roasted tomatoes, diced
- 4 c. chicken broth
- 3 sliced green onions
- For serving: Cooked white rice

Instructions:

Melt the butter in a deep pan on moderately low heat.

Add the flour to the pan, stirring often, and cook for ten minutes until it turns a dark caramel. Stir in onions, celery, and bell pepper; cook for 5 minutes longer until softened.

Add the sausage and garlic, stir to combine, and then stir in Cajun seasoning, pepper, and salt. Add the chicken broth, bay leaf, and diced tomatoes; allow to boil. Simmer on low for 1 hour, frequently stirring, until the mixture is thickened.

Add the shrimp during the last minute of cooking time until cooked through and pink. Stir in half of the green onions.

Top the mixture on your cooked rice. Sprinkle on top with green onions. Enjoy!

Chicken Étouffée

This Chicken Étouffée is an awesome lunch recipe for any occasion. I love eating it with fresh steamed rice and hot sauce. It's about as close to heaven for me as a person can get.

Servings: 6

Preparation Time: 30 minutes

Ingredients:

- 2 tbsp. butter
- 2 tbsp. oil
- 1 onion (peeled, chopped)
- 3 cloves garlic (minced)
- ½ stalk celery (chopped)
- 1 green bell pepper (finely chopped)
- ¼ c. flour
- ⅛ tsp. cayenne pepper
- 1½ tsp. Cajun seasoning
- 6 boneless skinless chicken breasts
- 1 (14 oz.) can chicken stock
- 1 (14 oz.) can chopped tomatoes
- 2 tbsp. tomato puree
- 1 lb. shrimp (peeled, deveined)
- White rice (for serving)

Instructions:

In a skillet, melt the butter with the oil over medium heat.

Add the onion, garlic, celery, and green pepper and stir well.

Using a bowl, mix the flour with the cayenne pepper and seasoning.

In the meantime, cut each of the chicken breasts into three pieces and dunk in your flour mixture.

Take the veggies out of the skillet and put them to one side on a dinner plate.

Add the coated fillets to the skillet followed by any leftover flour mixture, cook while stirring for 5 minutes until both are gently browned.

Return the veggies to the skillet together with the stock, chopped tomatoes, and tomato puree.

Bring to boil, before reducing the heat to a simmer, and simmer for 12-14 minutes, or until chicken cooks through completely and the sauce thickens.

Add the shrimp to the skillet, simmer for another 3-4 minutes, or until the shrimp curl and become pink.

Serve over white rice.

Louisiana Alligator Style Creole Stew

Alligator Creole Stew is a classic Cajun dish. With this recipe, I created an alligator creole stew recipe that's easy to make and tastes awesome. You'll be glad you tried it.

Servings: 12

Preparation Time: 1 hour and 15 minutes

Ingredients:

- 3 tbsp. canola oil
- 1 c. white wine
- 2 c. onions (peeled, diced)
- 4 tbsp. Minced garlic
- 1 ½ c. green bell peppers, diced
- 1 c. celery, diced
- 48 oz. canned tomatoes (diced)
- 3 c. potatoes (cut into medium dice)
- 2 tbsp. Dried thyme
- ¼ lb. butter
- 2 tbsp. Dried oregano
- 2 bay leaves
- ¼ tsp. cayenne
- 2 tsp. hot sauce
- 5 c. chicken stock
- 1 tsp. sauce, Worcestershire
- Pepper
- Salt
- 4 lb. Louisiana alligator (cut into 1" cubes)
- 2 c. chopped green onions
- 2 sliced French baguettes (toasted)

Instructions:

In a large (8-quart) stockpot over moderately high heat, heat the canola oil.

Add the garlic along with the celery, onions, and green bell peppers. Allow cooking for 8 minutes until onions become translucent, and the veggies are tender.

Pour in the white wine along with the chicken stock, and add the tomatoes, followed by the potatoes, oregano, cayenne, bay leaves, thyme, hot sauce, and Worcestershire sauce.

Taste, season, and bring to a simmer for about 5 minutes.

Add the alligator to the stew, and simmer for 45 minutes while covered.

Add the butter and chopped onions, stirring until well melted. Remove and discard the bay leaves.

Serve with toasted slices of French baguette.

Gumbo

Gumbo is a hugely popular stew in Louisiana, and it is, in fact, the state's official dish. It is thought to have originated in southern Louisiana in the 18th century and was introduced by the Choctaws.

Servings: 10-15

Preparation Time: 2 hours and 30 minutes

Ingredients:

- 20 c. chicken stock
- 1 lb. butter, unsalted
- 3 c. divided flour, all-purpose
- 2 diced red bell peppers
- 2 diced green bell peppers
- 2 small yellow onions (peeled, diced)
- 2 diced celery stalks
- 2 tbsp. Creole seasoning
- 1 tsp. black pepper, ground
- 1 tsp. hot red pepper flakes, dried
- 1 tsp. chili powder
- 2 bay leaves
- 1 tsp. thyme, dried
- 1 lb. sliced andouille sausage (¼" thick slices)
- 1 tbsp. garlic, chopped
- 2 tbsp. kosher salt
- 3½ lb. boned chicken (roasted)
- Hot sauce
- Boiled rice (to serve)

Instructions:

In an extra-large pot of around 12-quart capacity, over medium-low heat, melt the butter.

Gradually add around 1 c. of your flour, continually stirring with a spoon, and allow to cook for 30 seconds.

Add another c. of flour and constantly stir for 30 seconds.

Finally, add the third c. and continuously stir for 30 seconds.

Continue cooking the roux, constantly stirring, for between 45-60 minutes, until the roux is a dark mahogany color.

Add the bell pepper and continually stir for 30 seconds.

Add the onions followed by the celery, and once again, while continually stirring, cook for 30 seconds.

Add the chicken stock, Creole seasoning, black pepper, red pepper flakes, chili powder, dried thyme, garlic, bay leaves, kosher salt, and sausage and allow to boil.

Uncovered, simmer the gumbo for 45 minutes while occasionally stirring and skim off any surface fat.

Add the chicken and let simmer for 15 minutes.

Taste and season with the sauce.

Serve with rice.

Blackened Fish

My Blackened Fish Recipe is perfect for all types of barbeques and cookouts. The key to this recipe is the spice rub. Once you try it, you'll be hooked!

Servings: 4

Preparation Time: 20 minutes

Ingredients:

- 4 (4- to 6-oz.) catfish fillets
- ½ c. peanut oil
- 2 tbsp. Cajun Spice Blend
- 2 tsp. garlic salt

Instructions:

Prepare the grill with about 5 lb. of charcoal and heat until the coals are white, or preheat the gas grill to high. Place a cast-iron griddle or skillet over the coals or gas burner for 20 minutes until it is very hot.

Meanwhile, coat the catfish fillets with the peanut oil, then sprinkle with Cajun spice blend and garlic salt on both sides. Marinate for 20 minutes.

Cook for 5 minutes, until white, then flip and cook for 5 more minutes, until flaky. Serve immediately.

Cornbread Stuffed Pork Loin on the Grill

This is a simple, no-brain recipe. It's mostly hands-off and just takes some patience. You can watch it cooking on the grill or cook the cornbread first before putting the pork in. I prefer to cook it first and mix the cornbread stuffing afterward.

Servings: 6-8

Preparation Time: 2 hours and 15 minutes

Ingredients:

- 1 4-5 lb. center-cut pork loin
- ½ lb. smoked bacon, diced
- ¼ c. sweet cream butter
- ½ c. sweet yellow onions
- ½ c. celery, diced
- ½ c. poblano peppers, diced
- 4 cloves garlic, crushed and minced
- 1 1-lb. package cornbread stuffing mix
- 2 c. chicken stock
- 1 tsp. salt
- 1 tsp. black pepper
- 1 tsp. sage
- ¼ c. apple cider vinegar
- ½ c. brown sugar
- 3 tbsp. maple syrup
- 1 tbsp. Dijon mustard
- 2 tsp. crushed red pepper flakes
- 1 tsp. Cajun seasoning

Instructions:

Prepare an outdoor or large stovetop grill, with a cover, over medium heat.

Place a skillet directly over the heat and add the bacon. Cook until browned and crispy. Remove the bacon from the skillet and set it aside.

Add the butter to the bacon grease in the skillet.

Once the butter has melted, add the onion, celery, poblano peppers, and garlic. Sauté for 5 minutes.

Add the cooked bacon, stuffing mix, and chicken stock. Mix well, cover, and cook for 10-15 minutes, then remove the skillet from the heat and set it aside for 10 minutes.

Butterfly your pork loin and season with additional salt and black pepper, if desired.

Fluff the cornbread stuffing in the skillet with a fork, and place it in the center of the pork loin. Fold or roll the pork loin over and secure it using kitchen twine.

Place the pork loin on the grill, over indirect heat, and cover.

In a saucepan, combine the sage, apple cider vinegar, brown sugar, maple syrup, Dijon mustard, crushed red pepper flakes, and Cajun seasoning over medium heat.

Cook for 5 minutes, frequently stirring until the mixture begins to bubble and thicken.

Remove the sauce from the heat and generously glaze the pork loin.

Cook for 1 ½ hours, glazing every 10 minutes until the internal temperature of the pork reaches 165°F. This should take approximately 30 minutes.

Remove the pork loin from the grill and set it aside to rest for at least 10 minutes before slicing and serving.

Rabbit Smothered in Sauce

A southern favorite, this rabbit is smothered in a tomato-based sauce, covered with cheese.

Servings: 6-8

Preparation Time: 2 hours

Ingredients:

- 2 lb. rabbit, cut into pieces
- 1 c. milk
- 2 tsp. cayenne pepper sauce
- 1 tbsp. Cajun seasoning
- 2 c. flour
- 1 tsp. salt
- 1 tsp. coarsely ground black pepper
- 1 tsp. cayenne powder
- 1 tbsp. fresh thyme, chopped
- 1 tsp. onion powder
- ½ c. vegetable oil
- 1 c. red onion, chopped
- 1 c. celery, chopped
- 1 c. green bell pepper, chopped
- 4 cloves garlic, crushed and minced
- ½ c. tomatoes, chopped
- 2 c. mushrooms, quartered
- 3 c. chicken stock
- 1 fresh rosemary sprig
- 2 bay leaves
- ¼ c. fresh parsley, chopped

Instructions:

Place the rabbit pieces in a bowl or large food storage bag.

Combine the milk, cayenne pepper sauce, and Cajun seasoning. Mix well and pour over the rabbit.

Place it in the refrigerator and marinate overnight.

Remove the rabbit from the marinade and set it aside.

In a bowl, combine the flour, salt, black pepper, cayenne powder, thyme, and onion powder. Mix well.

Heat the vegetable oil in a deep skillet over medium heat.

Dredge the rabbit in the flour and place it into the hot skillet. If the rabbit is brown on both sides, remove it from the skillet and set it aside.

Add the onion, celery, and green bell peppers to the skillet. Then, cook for 5 minutes or until firm tender.

Put in the garlic, tomatoes, mushrooms, and chicken stock. Bring the mixture to a gentle boil.

Add the rabbit back into the skillet, along with the rosemary and bay leaves.

Reduce the heat to low, cover, and simmer for 1 ½ hours.

Remove from the heat. Remove the rosemary and bay leaves, and stir in the parsley right before serving.

Cheesy Shrimp and Grits

Shrimp and Grits are a southern favorite. This Cheesy Shrimp and Grits recipe is real good.

Servings: 6

Preparation Time: 40 minutes

Ingredients:

- 2 c. water
- 2 c. chicken broth (low-sodium)
- 1 c. corn grits
- 1 c. shredded cheddar
- 4 tbsp. butter
- Kosher salt
- Freshly ground black pepper
- 6 slices bacon
- 1 lb. peeled large shrimp, deveined
- 1/4 tsp. paprika
- 1 tsp. dried oregano
- 4 green onions, thinly sliced plus extra for garnishing
- 2 minced cloves garlic
- Juice of 1/2 lemon

Instructions:

Place the water and chicken broth in a medium saucepan and bring to a boil.

Season the mixture generously with salt and simmer on low, whisking in grits. Stir often and simmer for 10 minutes until your grits are soft and the liquid is absorbed.

Stir in cheese and butter; season with salt and pepper.

Cook the bacon in a large pan on medium heat for eight minutes. Drain on a plate lined with a paper towel, leaving two tbsp. bacon fat in the pan.

Chop the bacon into small bits. Season your shrimp using paprika and oregano.

Add the shrimp, garlic, and green onions to the skillet; cook and stir for 4 minutes until the shrimp is cooked thoroughly and pink in color. Add lemon juice to shrimp.

Place the grits on a serving platter and top the shrimp and chopped bacon.

Serve!

Cajun Brisket

Naturally, smoked beef cooking in its own juices or basted with a brown sauce is the type of brisket which can be found in a good Cajun kitchen.

Servings: 8

Preparation Time: 8 hours and 10 minutes

Ingredients:

- 1 beef brisket, approximately 5 lb.
- 1 tbsp. brown sugar
- 1 tbsp. onion powder
- 1 tbsp. garlic powder
- 1 tbsp. smoked paprika
- 1 tsp. cayenne powder
- 1 tbsp. fresh oregano, chopped
- 1 tbsp. fresh thyme chopped
- 1 tbsp. coarse sea salt
- 1 tbsp. coarsely ground black pepper
- 2 c. red bell pepper, sliced
- 2 c. green bell pepper, sliced
- 2 c. onions, sliced
- 4 c. stewed tomatoes, with liquid, chopped
- ½ c. tomato paste
- 1 c. stout style beer

Instructions:

In a bowl, combine the brown sugar, onion powder, garlic powder, smoked paprika, cayenne powder, oregano, thyme, sea salt, and black pepper. Mix well.

Generously pat the spice mixture all over the brisket. Cover the meat tightly in plastic wrap and place it in the refrigerator for 8 hours or overnight.

Remove the plastic wrap from the meat and place it in a large slow cooker.

Add the red bell peppers, green bell peppers, and onions around the meat.

Combine the stewed tomatoes, tomato paste, and stout-style beer. Pour this mixture over the meat and vegetables.

Cover the slow cooker and cook on low for 8 hours or until the brisket easily falls apart and it is tender.

Crispy Cajun Shrimp

This is a perfect recipe to whip up for the family on a Sunday afternoon. The breading is so spicy, and the shrimp are tender.

Servings: 4

Preparation Time: 30 minutes

Ingredients:

- 3 c. panko breadcrumbs
- 1 lb. shrimp, peeled, tail on or off
- 2 lightly beaten eggs, large
- 1 c. all-purpose flour
- 2 tsp. Cajun seasoning
- 2 c. vegetable oil or more

Instructions:

Over moderate heat in a large saucepan, heat the vegetable oil until hot.

Place the shrimp on a paper towel; pat them dry.

Season with the Cajun seasoning

Now, first, dip in the seasoned pieces of shrimp into the flour, then into the egg, and finally into the breadcrumbs.

Carefully place them into the hot oil & fry them until golden brown. Serve & enjoy.

Fried Soft Shell Crab

Softshell crabs are usually fried until crispy. This recipe is less messy and a lot easier to prepare.

Servings: 4

Preparation Time: 20 minutes

Ingredients:

- 6 soft shell crabs, cleaned
- 2 eggs, lightly beaten
- 1 tsp. onion powder
- Black pepper
- 1 c. whole milk
- ¼ c. tarragon vinegar
- 1 tbsp. Cajun seasoning
- 2 tsp. cayenne pepper sauce
- 1 tsp. salt
- 2 c. flour
- ½ c. cornstarch
- 1 tsp. paprika, smoked
- 1 tsp. powdered cayenne
- 1 tsp. thyme
- Vegetable oil for frying

Instructions:

Place the crabs in a large bowl or food storage bag.

Combine the eggs, milk, tarragon vinegar, Cajun seasoning, and cayenne pepper sauce together and pour it over the crabs. Cover and refrigerate for at least 30 minutes.

In a bowl, combine the flour, cornstarch, onion powder, smoked paprika, cayenne powder, thyme, salt, and black pepper. Mix well.

Place a deep skillet or frying pan on the stove and heat approximately 1 ½ inches of oil over medium-high heat.

Remove the crabs from the marinade and dredge each of them in the flour mixture.

Place them in the hot oil, taking care not to overcrowd them.

Cook for 3-4 minutes, or until a good amount of bubbles can be seen forming on the surface of the crabs. The color should be a deep golden brown.

Remove the crabs from the hot oil and set them on paper towels to drain before serving.

Dinner

Spend the night with wonderful dishes from Louisiana! The Dinner meal is always the fanciest and most flavorful meal of the day. Be sure to make one of these amazing recipes for your friends and family. They will love it!

Cajun Chicken

This Cajun Chicken recipe is a great way to spice up your dinner. It's low in calories and full of flavor.

Servings: 4

Preparation Time: 45 minutes

Ingredients:

- 2 tbsp. extra-virgin olive oil
- 1 c. diced red and green bell peppers
- 1 c. diced medium onion
- Freshly ground black pepper
- Kosher salt
- 4 boneless & skinless chicken breasts
- 1 c. shredded Cheddar
- 2 tbsp. Cajun seasoning

Instructions:

Preheat the oven to 350 degrees F.

Heat the oil in a large oven-resistant skillet set on moderate heat.

Add the bell peppers and onions to the skillet; cook for five minutes until soft. Season the mixture with salt and pepper; remove from heat to cool slightly.

Using a sharp knife, make a pocket in the chicken breast and stuff with the sautéed vegetable mixture.

Sprinkle with Cheddar and season with black pepper, Cajun seasoning, and pepper.

Place the chicken in the same skillet and bake for 25 minutes until well done.

Serve!

Cajun BBQ Chicken

BBQing is a truly American cooking method and Cajun BBQ Chicken is a perfect way to infuse it with the Cajun style.

Servings: 4

Preparation Time: 55 minutes

Ingredients:

- 1 tbsp. extra-virgin olive oil
- 1 lb. boneless & skinless chicken breast
- 1 tsp. dried oregano
- Freshly ground black pepper
- Kosher salt
- 1 tbsp. butter
- 2 minced cloves garlic
- 1/4 c. beer
- 1/2 c. barbecue sauce
- Juice of 1 lime
- 1 tbsp. Worcestershire sauce
- Dash of hot sauce
- 2 tsp. Cajun seasoning, divided
- Pinch of crushed red pepper flakes
- 1/4 c. sliced green onions
- Cooked rice, for serving

Instructions:

Heat the oil in a large skillet on medium heat.

Season the chicken breasts all over with oregano, 1 tsp. Cajun seasoning, salt, and pepper.

Place the chicken in the skillet; cook for six to eight minutes on each side until golden. Remove from heat and set aside.

Melt the butter in the same skillet and cook the garlic for 30 seconds until fragrant.

Stir in barbecue sauce, Worcestershire sauce, beer, red pepper flakes, lime juice, hot sauce, and remaining Cajun seasoning. Bring to a boil and simmer on low for five minutes.

Return the chicken to the skillet; simmer for additional 3-5 minutes.

Sprinkle the chicken with chopped green onions. Serve over cooked rice.

Enjoy!

Shrimp, Sausage, And Grits

This Shrimp, Sausage, And Grits recipe is southern comfort food at its best. It combines the flavors of Louisiana and eats like old-fashioned New Orleans family cooking.

Servings: 6

Preparation Time: 30 minutes

Ingredients:

- 4 c. Seafood Stock
- 1 c. grits (instant or 5-minute)
- ½ lb. Jarlsberg cheese or Swiss cheese, grated, divided
- 1 lb. andouille or smoked sausage, cut into ½-inch cubes
- 4 tbsp. (½ stick) unsalted butter
- 1 lb. button mushrooms, sliced
- 1 c. finely chopped scallions (white and green parts), divided
- 4 garlic cloves, minced
- ½ c. dry white wine
- 1 lb. shrimp, peeled and deveined
- ½ tbsp. Cajun Spice Blend
- ¼ c. grated Parmesan cheese

Instructions:

In a 2-quart saucepan, bring the seafood stock to a simmer over medium heat. Stir in the grits and bring to boil, then simmer, occasionally stirring, for 5 to 7 minutes. Fold in ¼ lb. or half of the Jarlsberg cheese and allow it to melt into the grits. Cover and set aside.

In a large sauté pan, cook the sausage on all sides over medium heat until browned. Transfer to a plate lined with paper towels. In the same pan, melt the butter, then add the mushrooms, ¾ c. of scallions, and the garlic and cook for 3 to 4 more minutes. Add the white wine, reduce the heat, and simmer for 1 to 2 minutes. Gently add the shrimp and the Cajun spice blend and stir well.

Fold in the sausage and stir in the remaining ¼ lb. of Jarlsberg cheese until well combined.

Sprinkle the remaining ¼ c. of scallions and the Parmesan cheese evenly over the top.

Divide the grits evenly among 6 plates, then spoon the shrimp and sausage sauce evenly over the grits. Serve immediately.

Shrimp And Andouille Dirty Rice

This dish is bursting with flavor and the result of a delicious combination. You'll find yourself rotating this one in your recipe rotation.

Servings: 6

Preparation Time: 50 minutes

Ingredients:

- 1½ tbsp. Creole Spice Blend
- 2 tsp. dry mustard
- 2 tsp. ground cumin
- 1 tbsp. unsalted butter
- ½ lb. ground chicken gizzards
- 4 oz. ground pork
- ½ lb. andouille sausage, diced
- 1½ c. Cajun Trinity
- 4 garlic cloves, minced
- 2 c. Chicken Stock
- ¾ c. uncooked converted white rice
- ½ lb. shrimp, peeled and deveined

Instructions:

In a small bowl, combine the Creole spice blend, dry mustard, and cumin and set aside.

In a large skillet, melt the butter over medium heat. Add the chicken gizzards, pork, and sausage and cook for 5 minutes, or until the meat is browned and no pink remains. Add the spice mixture, Cajun Trinity, and garlic, and stir well. Cook for 5 more minutes, frequently stirring until the Cajun Trinity is soft and translucent.

Add the chicken stock and rice, stir well, and bring to a boil. Reduce the heat to low, cover, and simmer for 15 minutes. Add the shrimp and stir well. Turn off the heat and keep the skillet on the stove, covered, for 10 more minutes, or until the rice is tender and the shrimp is pink.

Transfer to a casserole dish or bowl and serve immediately.

Cajun Shrimp Kebabs

These Cajun shrimp kebabs are a great way to spice up your dinner. They are easy and delicious.

Servings: 4-6

Preparation Time: 30 minutes

Ingredients:

- 2 tbsp. olive oil
- 1 lb. shrimp
- 1 tsp. cayenne
- 1 tsp. kosher salt
- 1 tsp. garlic powder
- 1 tsp. paprika
- 1 tsp. oregano
- 1 tsp. onion powder
- 2 lemons, sliced thinly crosswise

Instructions:

Heat up the grill to medium-high.

Combine in a small bowl the cayenne, salt, paprika, garlic powder, onion powder, and oregano, stirring until combined.

Toss the shrimp in olive oil and spice mix until coated well.

Thread the shrimp and lemon onto wooden skewers or metal skewers. If using wooden skewers, soak them for twenty minutes before using them.

Grill the skewered shrimp and lemon for 4 to 5 minutes, turning once halfway of cooking, or until the shrimp turns opaque and the lemon is charred.

Serve!

Fried Catfish Nuggets

These fried catfish nuggets are easy to make and delicious. They are a perfect meal for your family or a fun dinner for you and a friend.

Servings: 4-6

Preparation Time: 25 minutes

Ingredients:

- 2 lb. catfish nuggets
- 1 egg, lightly beaten
- 2 c. buttermilk
- 1 tsp. cayenne pepper sauce
- 2 ½ c. cornmeal
- 2 tsp. Cajun seasoning
- 1 tsp. salt
- 1 tsp. coarsely ground black pepper
- Vegetable oil for frying

Instructions:

Combine the egg, buttermilk, and cayenne pepper sauce in a bowl and mix well.

Add the catfish nuggets to the buttermilk mixture, toss to coat, and let them sit for 5-10 minutes.

In another bowl, combine the cornmeal, Cajun seasoning, salt, and black pepper. Adjust the seasonings to suit your own taste preferences.

In a deep skillet or deep fryer, add enough oil to completely submerge the catfish nuggets, approximately 1 ½ inches if using a skillet. Heat the oil over medium-high.

Remove the catfish nuggets from the buttermilk and toss in the cornmeal mixture to coat thoroughly.

Place the cornmeal-crusted catfish nuggets in the hot oil. Cook, occasionally turning for 5-7 minutes or until they are golden brown and flake easily.

Remove the catfish nuggets from the pan and let them drain on a paper towel before serving.

Buffalo Shrimp

A nice meal for dinner is Buffalo Shrimp. It's easy to prepare and can serve as a complete meal on its own. Or you can add it to your favorite Cajun recipe for an extra kick.

Servings: 4

Preparation Time: 6 minutes

Ingredients:

- 1 tsp. garlic powder
- 2 tbsp. Cajun seasoning
- 2 tsp. cayenne pepper
- 1 tsp. onion powder
- 1 lb. peeled and deveined shrimp
- Pepper to taste – use lots
- 1 c. flour
- 2 beaten eggs
- 3 c. vegetable oil
- 1 ½ c. Panko breadcrumbs

Buffalo Sauce:

- ¼ c. butter
- 5 minced garlic cloves
- 4 tbsp. hot pepper sauce
- 2 tbsp. orange juice

Instructions:

Combine the Cajun seasoning, garlic powder, onion powder, cayenne pepper, and pepper in a bowl.

Coat the shrimp with the spice mixture and refrigerate for 45 minutes.

Place the eggs in one dish, the flour in a second dish, and the breadcrumbs in a third dish.

Dredge the spiced shrimp through the eggs, flour, and breadcrumbs.

Combine the sauce ingredients in a pan and stir until combined, about 3 minutes. Set aside, but keep warm.

Heat the oil in a large skillet or deep fryer.

Fry the shrimp for 3 minutes.

Drain shrimp on a paper towel. Coat with the sauce.

Beer-Battered Cajun Fried Fish

Beer-Battered Cajun Fried Fish is a recipe that will soon become a family favorite. It's easy to prepare and bursting with flavor.

Servings: 4

Preparation Time: 10 minutes

Ingredients:

- 1 egg
- 1 c. beer
- ¾ c. flour
- ½ c. cornmeal
- 1 tsp. garlic salt
- Salt and pepper to taste
- 1 tsp. Cajun seasoning
- 1 lb. haddock fillets
- 4 c. vegetable oil

Instructions:

Whisk the egg, beer, flour, cornmeal, garlic salt, salt, pepper, and Cajun seasoning in a bowl

Coat the haddock fillets with the batter.

Let sit for 20 minutes.

Heat the oil in a large skillet and fry the fish for 5 minutes on each side until the haddock is flaky.

Court-Bouillon

Court-bouillon is a fish and seafood stew that originated from the Cajun area of Louisiana. Any species of fish can be added to it and it's a great way to add flavor to your seafood dishes.

Servings: 12

Preparation Time: 45 minutes

Ingredients:

- ½ c. olive oil
- ½ c. flour
- 1 small chopped onion
- 3 minced garlic cloves
- 2 chopped celery stalks
- 3 c. seafood stock
- 2 c. drained stewed tomatoes
- Salt and pepper to taste
- ½ tsp. hot sauce
- ½ tsp. Cajun seasoning
- 4 lb. tilapia fillets

Instructions:

Preheat the oven to 350 degrees.

Combine the olive oil and flour in a pan to create a roux.

Keep stirring for 10 minutes.

Stir in the onion, garlic, and celery and cook for 5 minutes.

Add the tomatoes and fish stock.

Season the fish with salt, pepper, hot sauce, and Cajun seasoning.

Place the tilapia in a baking dish in a single layer.

Cover the tilapia with the sauce.

Bake for 30 minutes. Serve over rice.

Cajun Beef Stew

This Cajun beef stew recipe is easy to make and bursting with flavor. It's another one of my family's favorites.

Servings: 6

Preparation Time: 3 hours and 5 minutes

Ingredients:

- 3 lb. stew meat
- ¼ c. flour
- 2 tbsp. Cajun seasoning
- Salt and pepper to taste
- 3 tbsp. olive oil
- ¼ c. red wine
- 2 lb. small potatoes, halved
- 2 chopped onions
- 4 chopped celery stalks
- 4 peeled and sliced carrots
- 5 c. beef broth
- 1 c. tomato sauce

Instructions:

Combine the flour with the Cajun seasoning, salt, and pepper.

Rub the mixture over the entire roast.

Heat the oil in a Dutch oven.

Brown the meat for 5 minutes on all sides.

Transfer the meat to a platter.

Scrape the brown bits with the wine.

Add the potatoes, celery, onion, and carrots.

Return the beef to the Dutch oven.

Pour in the broth and tomato sauce. Simmer the roast for 1 hour.

Southern Fried Chicken

This fried chicken recipe is a great southern dish that will soon become a family favorite. It's very easy to prepare and delicious. The skin on this fried chicken is unbelievably crisp.

Servings: 6

Preparation Time: 20 minutes

Ingredients:

- 3 lb. chicken breasts
- 3 beaten eggs
- ½ tsp. hot sauce
- 1 tsp. garlic powder
- 1 tsp. Cajun season or to taste
- ½ tsp. paprika
- ¾ buttermilk
- Salt and pepper to taste
- 1 c. flour
- ¼ c. cornstarch
- 1 c. lard or Crisco

Instructions:

Season the chicken lightly with some of the seasonings, salt, and pepper.

Combine the eggs, buttermilk, hot sauce, remaining seasonings, salt, and pepper in a bowl.

Heat the lard in a large skillet.

Add the flour and cornstarch to a bowl.

Dredge the chicken through the egg mixture, then the flour mixture.

Make sure the lard is hot enough.

Cook the chicken for 20 minutes while turning the pieces once or twice.

Parmesan-Crusted Pork Chops

This parmesan-crusted pork chop recipe is easy to make and has just the right amount of spice.

Servings: 2

Preparation Time: 50 minutes

Ingredients:

- 1 egg
- ½ tsp. Worcestershire sauce
- ¼ c. grated Parmesan cheese
- ¼ c. Panko breadcrumbs
- ½ tsp. garlic powder
- 1 tsp. Cajun seasoning
- 2 thick pork chops

Instructions:

Preheat the oven to 350 degrees.

Coat a baking dish with non-stick spray.

Whisk the egg with the Worcestershire sauce

Combine the grated cheese, breadcrumbs, garlic powder, and Cajun seasoning in a bowl.

Dredge the pork chops through the egg mixture, then the cheese/breadcrumb mixture.

Transfer the chops to the baking dish. Bake for 50 minutes until the pork chops are done.

Creole Okra Shrimp

This Creole Okra Shrimp recipe is a good way to make okra more accessible to your family. It's easy to prepare and has a delicious flavor.

Servings: 4

Preparation Time: 35 minutes

Ingredients:

- 1 lb. de-veined, peeled shrimp, large
- 3/4 c. celery, sliced diagonally
- 1 c. onion, sliced vertically
- 2 c. trimmed, halved okra, fresh
- 1 1/2 tbsp. of oil, olive
- 1 c. milk, reduced fat
- 1 c. grits
- 3 c. chicken stock, unsalted
- 2 sliced green onions
- 1 1/2 tbsp. of vinegar, red wine
- 1/2 c. water, filtered
- 1 bay leaf
- 3 chopped cloves of garlic
- 3 c. marinara sauce, fresh
- 1/2 tsp. salt, kosher
- 1/2 tsp. black pepper, ground
- 1/2 tsp. red pepper, ground

Instructions:

Bring the stock, bay leaf, milk, and garlic to boil in a large-sized saucepan on med-high. Add 1/4 tsp. of salt and then grits. Stir constantly using a whisk.

Reduce the heat to med-low. Cook for 20 minutes, occasionally stirring. The mixture should thicken. Discard the bay leaf. Cover the pan and keep it warm.

Heat large-sized skillet on high. Add the oil and swirl around the pan to coat evenly. Add celery, okra, and onion and cook without stirring for two to four minutes. Veggies should brown.

Add the last 1/4 tsp. of salt, plus red and black pepper and shrimp. Cook for two minutes while occasionally stirring. Stir in 1/2 c. of water and the sauce. Bring to simmer. Then, cook for three minutes. Shrimp should be done. Add vinegar and stir.

Place 1/2 c. of grits each in four bowls. Top Servings with 1 & 1/2 c. of shrimp mixture each. Evenly sprinkle with the green onions. Serve.

Creole Collard Greens

Another southern dish you'll want to make again and again. With this Creole Collard Greens recipe, collards take on a new magical twist thanks to the spices and herbs.

Servings: 4-6

Preparation Time: 3 hours and 30 minutes

Ingredients:

- 2 quarts warm chicken broth
- 1 ham hock, smoked
- 2 bay leaves
- 4 smashed cloves of garlic
- 1 sliced onion
- 3 tbsp. oil, olive
- 2 bags collard greens, pre-washed and trimmed
- 1 tsp. sugar, granulated
- 2 tbsp. vinegar, apple cider
- Salt, kosher
- Black pepper, ground

Instructions:

Place the large stockpot on med heat. Add oil. When the oil has heated, add the ham hock, garlic, onion, and bay leaves.

Cook mixture till the onions soften and begin browning.

Pack in the collard greens. Push them into a pot. Add sugar, broth, and vinegar. Bring to boil and turn greens occasionally as they are wilting.

Lower heat to simmer. Cover pot. Cook for an hour. Taste broth. Add salt and/or pepper and adjust seasoning if desired.

Cover pot again. Allow cooking for two or two and a half more hours.

Remove ham hock and bay leaves. Dice them up and add back ham hock meat. Drain off any excess liquids from cooking. Serve.

Oyster Bacon Gumbo

This oyster bacon gumbo recipe is a great combination of flavors. It really adds a beautiful twist to the traditional Cajun dish.

Servings: 7-9

Preparation Time: 2 hours and 50 minutes

Ingredients:

- 6 minced cloves of garlic
- 2 chopped bell peppers
- 3 chopped stalks of celery
- 1 1/4 c. flour, all-purpose
- 2 chopped onions, large
- 1 lb. chopped bacon, thick-cut, smoked
- 4 quarts of chicken broth, unsalted
- Creole seasoning
- 2 quarts Louisiana oysters, shucked, in liquor
- To garnish: green onions

Instructions:

Cover the raw oysters. Chill until you need them.

Place the oyster liquor on med heat. Bring to a low boil. Simmer till liquid is reduced by 1/2. Skim off foam from the surface.

Add the chicken broth. Bring to a low boil. Turn burner off. Keep warm till needed.

Brown the bacon in a large-sized skillet on med-high. Remove the bacon. Reserve.

Measure 1/2 c. of bacon grease into skillet. Add oil if you need to. Add the onions and sauté till browned lightly. Sprinkle with flour evenly. Stir and break up lumps.

Reduce the heat to med. Cook for 10-20 minutes till the mixture is dark brown. Often stir so that it will not burn.

Add reserved bacon, garlic, bell pepper, and celery, and sauté for five minutes. Add 1 c. of warm broth slowly and stir vigorously. Repeat this step three times until the roux is dissolved.

Add the rest of the broth. Stir till the mixture is blended well. Bring to a low boil on med heat.

Reduce the heat to low. Simmer for an hour. Stir along the bottom of the pot to prevent the roux from settling. Then skim off foam and fat if they accumulate on the surface.

Taste the gumbo. Adjust the flavor with the Creole seasoning.

Add the reserved oysters and stir well. Return to a low boil for a couple of minutes as you stir it. Remove from burner. Allow standing for 8-10 minutes. Garnish with green onions. Serve hot with French bread.

Red Snapper

Red Snapper is a delicate fish with a buttery, slightly sweet flavor. Although the Cajun style of cooking is mostly associated with meat dishes, it lends quite nicely to fish dishes as well.

Servings: 8-10

Preparation Time: 1 hour and 10 minutes

Ingredients:

- 4 lb. snapper fillets
- 2 de-seeded, minced bell peppers, green
- 2 peeled, minced onions
- 1 peeled, crushed clove of garlic
- 1/4 lb. minced mushrooms, fresh
- 6 peeled tomatoes
- 2 tbsp. oil, olive
- 1 tbsp. parsley
- 1 c. wine, white
- 1 sprig saffron

Instructions:

Cook the garlic, mushrooms, peppers, and onions in oil for several minutes. Add the tomatoes. Cook on med-low for 1/2 hour. Add the saffron.

Arrange the fish in a buttered baking dish.

Pour wine over the fish. Season lightly using kosher salt and ground pepper.

Add the sauce and bake for 1/2 hour in a 350-degree F oven. Use parsley to garnish. Serve.

Cajun Honey Chicken Wings

These Cajun honey chicken wings are amazing. The wings and sauce are bursting with flavor, and the bones are easily picked out.

Servings: 32

Preparation Time: 55 minutes

Ingredients:

- 3 lb. chicken wings
- 1/3 c. Cajun seasoning
- 1 c. barbecue sauce
- 2 tbsp. honey
- 1 tbsp. sriracha sauce
- 1 lime, fresh

Instructions:

Preheat the oven to 350 degrees. Grease two large baking sheets with cooking spray.

Place the chicken wings onto the two baking sheets—season with the Cajun seasoning.

Place into the oven to bake for 30 minutes.

In a small bowl, add in one tbsp. of lime zest, juice from half of a lime, barbecue sauce, honey, and sriracha sauce. Whisk to mix.

Remove from the oven and baste with half of the sauce. Place back into the oven to bake for 10 minutes. Remove and baste again with the sauce. Place back into the oven to bake for an additional 10 minutes.

Remove and serve immediately.

Cajun Salmon

Stuffed salmon is bursting with flavor and can be served in many different ways. It's one of the best recipes in this book.

Servings: 4

Preparation Time: 20 minutes

Ingredients:

- 1 salmon fillet, boneless
- 2 tsp. creole seasoning
- 2 tsp. black pepper
- 2 tsp. powdered garlic
- 2 tsp. powdered onion
- 1 tsp. smoked paprika
- Dash of cayenne pepper
- 1 lemon, juice and zest only
- ¼ c. Italian parsley, minced
- 3 tbsp. extra virgin olive oil

Instructions:

Preheat the oven to 475 degrees F.

In a small bowl, add in the creole seasoning, black pepper, powdered garlic, powdered onion, cayenne pepper and smoked paprika. Stir well to mix.

Rinse the salmon under cold water. Pat dry with a few paper towels. Season the salmon on both sides with the seasoning mixture.

Transfer the seasoned salmon fillet into a large baking dish. Top off with the fresh lemon juice and lemon zest.

Place into the oven to bake for 10 to 12 minutes.

Remove and serve with a garnish of parsley.

Cajun Seared Scallops

Seared scallops are bursting with flavor and can be served many different ways. All will be pleased to get this dish in their collection.

Servings: 4

Preparation Time: 15 minutes

Ingredients:

- 1 lb. sea scallops
- 2 tsp. Cajun seasoning
- ½ tbsp. butter
- ½ tbsp. olive oil
- 1 clove garlic, chopped
- ½ c. heavy whipping cream
- 2 tsp. Cajun mustard
- 1 tbsp. lemon juice
- Dash of black pepper and salt
- 1 tbsp. parsley, chopped

Instructions:

Pat the scallops dry with a few paper towels. Season with the Cajun seasoning.

Set a skillet over medium-high heat. Pour in olive oil and butter and heat. Once the butter is melted, add in the scallops. Sear for 1 to 2 minutes on each side or until golden brown.

Add the garlic and let cook until fragrant for about 1 extra minute.

Mix in the heavy whipping cream, Cajun mustard, and fresh lemon juice. Stir well to mix and allow the mixture to boil. Reduce the heat to low. Simmer until you have a thick consistency for about 2 to 3 minutes.

Season with black pepper and salt.

Remove from heat and serve immediately with the chopped parsley.

Conclusion

After reading through this book, I hope you have learned everything you need to know about the Cajun culture. You'll be amazed at what they eat, how they cook it, and how a family is at the heart of it all.

As you can see, you're cooking has never been easier! With easy-to-follow recipes that will have your taste buds coming back for more, you'll soon be the master of your kitchen. I hope you found this book as helpful as I did.

Cajun cooking is famous for being spicy and flavorful. I'm sure that after reading this book, your belly will be burning to try some of their recipes. It's easy to prepare and bursting with flavor.

After reading through this book, you will experience the Cajun culture and learn everything you need to know about it. I hope you have enjoyed it and will take some time to try these recipes. Your family and friends will love them!

Thank you for purchasing my book.

Author's Afterthoughts

With so many books out there to choose from, I want to thank you for choosing this one and taking precious time out of your life to buy and read my work. Readers like you are the reason I take such passion in creating these books.

It is with gratitude and humility that I express how honored I am to become a part of your life and I hope that you take the same pleasure in reading this book as I did in writing it.

Can I ask one small favour? I ask that you write an honest and open review on Amazon of what you thought of the book. This will help other readers make an informed choice on whether to buy this book.

My sincerest thanks,

Angel Burns

If you want to be the first to know about news, new books, events and giveaways, subscribe to my newsletter by clicking the link below

https://angel-burns.gr8.com

or Scan QR-code

Made in United States
Orlando, FL
26 November 2024